I'm Just Feeling Upset and Frustrated

Amy Nnajiofor

To order additional copies of this book, contact:
Xlibris
1-800-455-039
www.xlibris.com.au
Orders@Xlibris.com.au

David & Opal Social Stories

I'm Just Feeling Upset and Frustrated

Amy Nnajiofor

David and Opal are best friends. They play together at school every day.

One day it was raining outside at school. David and Opal decided to play inside the classroom.

Opal decided to play her favourite musical instrument the guitar.

But David wanted to play with the guitar as well.

David walked over to Opal and took the guitar right out of her hands.

David did not use his manners. David did not ask if he could have a turn at playing the guitar. David just took the guitar from Opal.

13

Opal got really upset and frustrated with David for taking the guitar.

15

Opal walked over to David and hit him in the arm. Opal wanted to let David know she was feeling upset and frustrated.

17

David saw how upset and frustrated Opal was. David decided to give the guitar back to Opal.

David apologized to Opal for taking the guitar.

Opal apologised to David for hitting him in the arm. Opal told David that she hit him because she was feeling upset and frustrated.

23

David and Opal agreed to share the guitar. David and Opal each had a turn at playing the guitar.

Which answer is correct A B C

When do you think it is ok to hit your friends?

(A) It is never ok to hit your friends

(B) It is ok to hit your friends if you are feeling upset or frustrated.

(C) It is ok to hit your friends if they take the toy you are playing with.

The correct answer is A

It is never ok to hit your friends.

Reflection
What did we learn today?

It was wrong of David to take the guitar from Opal without asking.

David should have used his manners and asked Opal if he could have a turn playing the guitar.

Hitting our friends is never ok

We do not hit our friends if we are feeling upset or frustrated.

We do not hit our friends if they take a toy without asking.

Reflection

If we hit our friends they might hit us back.

If we hit our friends they might not want to be our friends anymore.

If we hit our friends they might not want to play with us.

If we hit our friends we could injure them or hurt their feelings.

We must keep our hands and feet to ourselves.

What do you think Opal could have done differently when David took her toy?

Reflection

Opal could have asked David to give back her toy.

Opal could have offered to share the toy with David.

Opal could have told an adult that David had taken her toy.

Let's agree to share with our friends. We want our friends to feel safe and happy.

Printed in the United States
By Bookmasters